LifeCaps Presents:

Grace Kelly of Monaco

The Inspiring Story of How An American Film Star Became a Princess

By Jennifer Warner

BookCaps™ Study Guides

www.bookcaps.com

© 2014. All Rights Reserved.

Table of Contents

About LifeCaps

LifeCaps is an imprint of BookCaps™ Study Guides. With each book, a lesser known or sometimes forgotten life is recapped. We publish a wide array of topics (from baseball and music to literature and philosophy), so check our growing catalogue regularly (**www.bookcaps.com**) to see our newest books.

Introduction

She has been called America's princess – and
with good reason. Long before she married a
prince, Grace Kelly had the looks and bearing of
royalty.

Born and raised in Philadelphia, the daughter of
an Irish Catholic father and a German immigrant
mother, Grace's blend of blonde-haired, blue-
eyed beauty and poise was dubbed a "snow-
covered volcano" by director Alfred Hitchcock.
Grace's co-star in the Hitchcock classic *Rear
Window*, actor Jimmy Stewart, observed: "How
could Hitch not help but fall in love with Grace?
Everyone loved her."

Yet, despite her beauty, Grace often seemed shy
and distant. "Since she was so beautiful, men
were always flirting with her," said costume
designer Edith Head, who designed her clothes
for the films she did with Hitchcock. "She wasn't
especially comfortable with such superficiality."

Grace didn't take herself too seriously. She even quipped in a few interviews that when 1950s movie powerhouses such Ava Gardner, Lana Turner or Elizabeth Taylor got into a taxi, the drivers always knew at once who they were, but when she got in cab, she was "always someone who looks like Grace Kelly."

Grace also had a sense of confidence in her femininity long before the era of women's liberation was ever in the headlines. She was often described by co-stars as focused and disciplined as an actress, yet also very approachable and easy to be around. Even later, when she became the center of attention, as a future royal, Grace sometimes seemed bemused and even caught off guard by all the attention.

Although Grace Kelly's film career spanned just 11 feature films over the course of five years, she made an indelible impact on Hollywood and the rest of the world. By looking at some of the many photos available of Grace on the Internet or by watching one of her 11 films, you cannot help but be struck by her innate sense of style and by her classic, seemingly effortless beauty. Always on the world's "most beautiful" and "best dressed" lists, Grace offers us a glimpse of glamor that is always just beyond our reach. Despite the fact that her last motion picture was released 58 years ago, her style, and, yes, her grace, remain as fresh and intriguing as ever.

But like most icons, there is more to Grace than what you see in film. While on the surface, she appeared to have lived a real-life fairy tale filled with handsome men, beautiful clothes and an adoring public, in reality, her life seems to have been more often a sad reflection of the times in which she lived. It was a time of movie megastars, of hushed-up love affairs, of prejudice and gossip, and of images not always being what they appeared to be.

Long before the world admired Kate Middleton's sophisticated sense of style, and long before the world fell in love with young Lady Diana's shy smile, there was a breathtakingly beautiful princess from Philadelphia. Her name was Grace Kelly, and this is her story.

Chapter 1: Early Life

Grace Patricia Kelly was born in Philadelphia on November 12, 1929, the third of four children of parents John Brendan "Jack" Kelly and Margaret Katherine Majer Kelly. She was named Grace after her father's sister, who died at a young age and also, she once told an interviewer, because of the nursery rhyme verse "Tuesday's child is full of grace" as she was born on a Tuesday.

Jack Kelly was a larger than life kind of man, and he was a big influence – both good and bad -- on young Grace. A local hero in Philadelphia, Jack Kelly was a three-time Olympic gold medalist as a sculler (rower) – the first to achieve that status in the sport -- and he instilled the importance of physical fitness and the love of sports in his children.

Jack Kelly was the best sculler in the United States when he joined the United States Army in 1916 as a private. While in the Army, he entered a boxing tournament as a heavyweight and ran up a 12-0 record before suffering a broken ankle.

Following his Army discharge as a lieutenant in in 1918, Jack returned home to Philadelphia where he continued his dominance in the sport of rowing, and he also played professional football for the Holmesburg Athletic Club, a team that won back-to-back city championships. In a 1919 game, Jack scored three touchdowns in just the first quarter of the game.

A savvy self-promoter, Jack also started his own brickwork contracting company in his hometown and through his slogan "Kelly for Brickwork" that cropped up around town at various building sites, and through his unusual technique for getting payment for his work, he was on his way to becoming a self-made millionaire.

To ensure he got paid for his work, Jack instructed his crews to mortar a single pane of glass into each chimney they constructed. When new home owners complained about smoke from their fireplaces backing into their houses, real estate developers would then pass the complaint on to Kelly. He would tell them he would take care of the problem once he got paid. After getting paid, a member of Jack's crew would drop a brick down the chimney, breaking the glass and solving the problem.

Jack was active in Philadelphia politics. He served as chairman of the Philadelphia County Democratic Party, and lost a very closely contested bid for mayor in 1935. Later in his career, he was a member of the Fairmount Park Commission and President Franklin Roosevelt named him National Director of Physical Fitness.

Grace's mother, Margaret Katherine Majer, was born in Schloss Helmsdorf, Germany, but she and her two siblings grew up in the Strawberry Mansion section of Philadelphia. Like her husband, Margaret Kelly was also a health and fitness buff.

A strong and robust-looking woman, Margaret's features include the strong angles and broad smile that she passed down to her daughter. She studied physical education at Temple University and later became the first woman to head the Physical Education Department at the University of Pennsylvania. As an undergraduate at Temple University, Margaret distinguished herself in intercollegiate swimming and was in a leadership positions with other female students as they played other sports at the Kingsessing facility that was used as a gymnasium at nearby University of Pennsylvania. After graduating from Temple in 1921, Margaret became the first coach of women's athletic teams at the University, founding a women's basketball team, scheduling the first intercollegiate competitions for women and then, three years later, establishing the institution's women's athletics program.

It was from Margaret, who worked as a photographer's model to help support herself in college, that Grace also got her comfort in front of the camera. Grace was to later say that "Ma" Kelly also instilled in her children this advice: "Be just, be punctual, buy only what you need and pay cash."

When Grace was born, the Kelly family already included two children, Margaret (Peggy), born in 1925 and John (Kell) Brendan, Jr., born in 1927. Another daughter, Elizabeth Anne (Lizanne) completed the family three and a half years after Grace was born.

"My father had a very simple view of life: you don't get anything for nothing," Grace once recalled in an interview. Jack Kelly, who, at a physically fit 6'2" in his prime, also certainly had a charming way about him and, always the consummate self-promoter and politician; he had a way of earning other people's trust.

Jack, however, did show definite opinions about his children. He made it clear to his family and friends that Peggy was his favorite, and it was a painful message that seemed to stay with Grace throughout her life.

Grace did not enjoy being the middle sister of the family. She often admitted that she grew up with the idea that she felt she could not compete for her parents' attention with Peggy, with her brother – the only boy of the family – and with Lizanne, the baby of the family.

It appears Jack did little to discourage Grace's feelings of being not good enough for his love and support. "I thought it would be Peggy whose name would be up in lights one day. Anything that Grace could do, Peggy could do better," he unabashedly told McCall's Magazine in a January, 1955 interview shortly before his by-then famous second daughter won the Academy Award for Best Actress for *The Country Girl.*

As an Irish American in the early part of the 20th century, even being a self-made business man couldn't buy Jack Kelly the social acceptance he craved. When he was kept from competing in England's prestigious Diamond Sculls at Henley because he "worked with his hands," for example, he sought to find vindication elsewhere – through hard work, politics and his family. His son, Kell, helped to avenge his father by becoming a championship rower himself, winning not only the Diamond Sculls but just about every single sculls championship in the world.

Friends of the family said the pressure Jack put on his children was not often healthy. "John Kelly expected a great deal from his kids," Grace's friend Rita Gam said simply.

Grace's brother, Kell, followed in his father's footsteps in several ways. He also became an Olympic sculler, winning a bronze medal in the 1956 Summer Olympics, and serving as a city councilman.

Grace Kelly enjoyed playing field hockey and basketball in school and was a lifelong swimmer -- she would later install a pool in the palace at Monaco -- but she did not consider herself an athlete. She preferred to dance, to read and to study theatrical arts. Her sister, Peggy, insisted in several later interviews that Grace wasn't shy like many studio-generated articles portrayed her, but that she was just quiet and often kept to herself as a child.

Whatever the case, young Grace seemed to feel she was a disappointment to her parents, and she felt she was somewhat of an outsider within her own family. Her lifelong friend, Rita Gam, admitted in an interview that Jack Kelly just wasn't interested in anyone who wasn't interested in sports.

Although it is hard to believe from looking at the family's old photos, Grace was not considered a beauty as a child or as a young teenager, and later she said she suffered from a painful lack of self confidence. She told biographer Robert Lacey, "I almost crawled into the woodwork I was so self-conscious. I was so bland; they kept having to introduce me again and again before people noticed me."

A favorite Kelly family story told how Lizanne once locked Grace locked in a cupboard. Instead of crying to be let out as most children would do, Grace stayed quietly locked in the dark cupboard for hours, talking to and playing with her dolls.

As an explanation for the oft-told family story, Lizanne later said Grace was born with a certain sense of serenity that the rest of the family simply did not possess. Peggy also was fond of mentioning to reporters that Grace told her that she going to become a princess one day.

Raised a Catholic, Grace attended the exclusive Catholic Ravenhill Academy in East Falls, Pennsylvania. She was reserved, quiet and even a bit gawky as a young girl, but she seemed to find herself on stage. Grace participated in school plays and community productions.

In the annual Ravenhall Christmas pageants, she progressed from the roles of shepherd, to angel, to Mary over her childhood years. In 1942, at the age of 12, she played a lead in a production of the play *Don't Feed the Animals*, produced by the East Falls Old Academy Players. For high school, Grace attended Stevens School, a secular academy. Her senior yearbook listed her favorite actress as Ingrid Bergman and her favorite actor as Joseph Cotten, a stage and film actor, who was interestingly enough an early Alfred Hitchcock favorite and the "Stevens' Prophecy" section predicted "Miss Grace P. Kelly – a famous star of stage and screen."

Grace may have gotten her love for acting and the arts in general from her beloved Uncle George, her father's older brother. Somewhat estranged from the family, possibly because of his homosexuality, George was a dramatist, screenwriter and director who penned a hit comedy-drama, *The Show Off*, in 1924 and was awarded the 1926 Pulitzer Prize for Drama for his play *Craig's Wife*. She later recalled many happy visits with her uncle listening with rapt attention to his stories of the entertainment world.

After graduating from Stevens School in May 1947, Grace decided to move to New York City despite her parents' objections. In fact, "objection" may be too light a word for how Jack felt about his daughter becoming an actress. Jack Kelly seemed proud to shock Grace's friends by calling the profession of acting a small cut above streetwalker.

Grace was determined, however, and she applied to the American Academy of Dramatic Arts in the hopes of becoming a stage actress. She took her audition piece from her Uncle George's 1923 play *The Torch-Bearers*. Admissions officers at the Academy of Dramatic Arts noted Grace's voice as "nasal" and "improperly placed." Even though Grace took speech classes and worked on her vocal tones along with the help of a tape recorder while she was at the Academy, many directors and casting agents still found Grace's voice unusual.

By this time, Grace had left any traces of her awkward childhood and teen years far behind, and her stunning good looks began to turn heads wherever she went. To pay for her room and board at Manhattan's Barbizon Hotel for Women, which prohibited men from entering after 10 p.m., Grace looked for work as a part-time model.

Her classic beauty and stately bearing earned her well-paid appearances in ads for Old Gold cigarettes and as the cover girl for popular national magazines such as Cosmopolitan and Redbook. Her modeling jobs paid amazingly well. Old Gold paid her $2,000 (roughly $20,000 in today's prices) for one session, for instance. She also did a few early TV commercials, including one for a bug spray which she said later required her to run around "smiling like an idiot and spraying like a demon."

Grace had a close circle of friends in New York. In fact, her good friend Rita Gam recalled in a 1983 interview, "She was a great woman's woman. She loved to giggle; she loved girl talk." To outsiders, however, Grace began to develop a bit of a reputation as being cold and distant.

She had a business-like demeanor, fellow students explained, and she had a way of distancing herself from. Academy student Mary Wolverton told biographer Robert Lacey. "There were students who were in awe of her because of her beauty and that distant quality she had.... She was so beautiful. But I always thought she was kind of cold."

That aloofness – combined with her exquisite beauty – came to serve her well on stage and on screen; in fact, it was just what Alfred Hitchcock loved about her.

Grace's final stage role as a student at the American Academy of Dramatic Arts was Tracy Lord in *The Philadelphia Story*. Ironically, she would reprise the role as a bona fide movie star in the 1956 film *High Society*.

Now 19, Grace was hoping to make it big on Broadway. "She had huge ambitions to become one of the fine stage actresses in America – that's what she wanted more than anything else. Her film work became just a detour," said Rita Gam. The fact that Grace never bought a home in Los Angeles, and worked extensive commuter time to New York City into her studio contract also showed her intentions for a future in stage work.

An early actor's bio Grace wrote for a role she played at the Bucks County Playhouse in New Hope, Pennsylvania, shows more about her upbringing than her bright future:

Grace Kelly: She is the daughter of John B. Kelly, of Philadelphia. Her brother recently figured in the news by winning the Diamond Sculls at the Henley Regatta in England. Her father was a champion oarsman and is well known as the former chairman of the Democratic Party in Philadelphia.

Grace worked in several theaters in New York, and performed with Raymond Massey in the August Strindberg play *The Father* before signing with agent Edith Van Cleve. She studied with the renowned acting teacher Sanford Meisner at the Neighborhood Playhouse in New York and worked summer stock in Colorado until Van Cleve, realizing Grace's potential for film work, suggested she try television.

Television producer Delbert Mann cast Grace as Bethel Merriday, an adaptation of the Sinclair Lewis novel of the same name, in her first television role. Between the years 1950 and 1951, when television was in its infancy and looking for new talent, the young actress performed in nearly 60 teleplays in New York City.

A 1952 article in Life Magazine describes the life of Grace the busy TV actress: "In one hectic 13-day period she played three roles: a college girl on Tuesday, a rich girl on Sunday and, eight days later, a country schoolteacher."

Although she was usually cast as the wholesome ingénue in these teleplays, she did foreshadow her talent for the murder-suspense plots Hitchcock enjoyed placing her in, by playing a few roles in the mystery-thriller series *Lights Out.*

Grace's voice, which she kept working hard to strengthen, may have kept her from becoming a stage success. Don Richardson, one of her directors and teachers later told biographer Robert Lacey that she had "no vocal horsepower." Whether that assessment was true or not, it was clear that the camera loved Grace.

Photographer Cecil Beaton explained it in a nuts-and-bolts kind of way: "She has, most important of all, a nice nose for photography: flat, it hardly exists at all in profile." He also commented on her square face and the square jaw that Grace said she initially tried to hide in photos and then came to embrace as a good feature.

Film also seemed to work well for the tall, slim actress, who was often told by theater casting directors that she was too tall. She was 5'7" in a sea of more diminutive actresses.

Grace's parents both believed her acting career would be short-lived, and Jack was especially patronizing of Grace's talents. When asked in later years about his sister's success, her brother, Kell, replied that is was in part due to the fact that she "got away from home early."

"None of the rest of us managed to do that," he explained.

Chapter 2: Acting Career

Grace's success on TV soon brought her to the silver screen. Her film debut was in a small role in the 1951 film *Fourteen Hours*. While the film did not receive any critical attention, she did catch the eye of Hollywood star Gary Cooper, who recommended the young actress to producer Stanley Kramer for a co-starring role his upcoming western *High Noon.*

Cooper called Grace different from other actresses with whom he had worked. Kramer sent Grace a telegram asking her to do the role while she was performing on stage in Colorado's Elitch Gardens. *High Noon* (1952), in which Grace played Cooper's young wife, was the first in an incredible string of plum film roles that landed Grace firmly in Hollywood as a star. The film also launched Grace's less than flattering reputation as a seductress of her leading men.

Grace's next film role co-starring with Clark Gable and Ava Gardner in 1953's *Mogambo*, a film shot on location in Kenya. Director John Ford had first noticed Grace in a screen test she took in 1950 and asked MGM to fly her to Los Angeles for an audition for his film in 1952. Ford said Kelly showed "breeding, quality and class" and offered her the role of Linda Nordley, which had originally been given to Gene Tierney. Grace also won a seven-year contract with MGM at the salary of $850 a week.

Still hoping for a stage career, Grace signed the deal under the conditions that she have one out of every two years off to work in the theater and that she be able to live in New York City. Grace later told columnist Hedda Hopper in an interview: "*Mogambo* had three things that interested me. John Ford, Clark Gable and a trip to Africa with expenses paid. If *Mogambo* had been made in Arizona, I wouldn't have done it."

Her work in *Mogambo* earned Grace a Golden Globe Award for Best Supporting Actress, her first Academy Award nomination for Best Supporting Actress and served to cement her off-screen image as well. Later, when asked about her affair with Gable, who was 28 years her senior, Grace reportedly said, "What else is there to do if you're alone in a tent in Africa with Clark Gable?"

The Hollywood talk about the aging star Gable and the young starlet certainly did not hurt ticket sales, and *Mogambo* was a huge box office success. Grace next starred in a teleplay called *The Way of an Eagle* with Jean-Pierre Aumont before she was cast in Alfred Hitchcock's film adaptation of Frederick Knott's Broadway hit *Dial M for Murder* opposite Ray Milland. Grace's role of Nancy, the wife of scheming naval officer Harry (Holden), proved to be a minor but pivotal part of the story, and it earned Grace notice with the critics. Her off-screen affair with the married Milland, however, caused Hedda Hopper to label Grace a nymphomaniac. It was a label that was to follow her for the rest of her life and is still part of any discussion of her legacy.

Much has been written about Grace's love life. If you read some accounts, it seems as if she had an affair with almost every man in Hollywood. "We were together a lot," her close friend Maree Rambo told Vanity Fair magazine years later in her defense, "and that was just not her style."

Grace's behavior was likely influenced by the way she was brought up and by what she witnessed as a child as she grew as part of the well-known Kelly family of Philadelphia. Wendy Leigh, author of *True Grace: The Life and Times of an American Princess*, explained, "Margaret was a healthy German blonde with no shame about her body. And then Grace's father was a great philanderer, so that she had the measure very early on about male animal instinct."

Other biographers have claimed that Grace's promiscuity may have been a rebellion against her father. Some writers feel she sought the relationships of older men as a sub-conscious way of seeking the love, support and approval she never got from Jack.

Grace herself admitted to writer Donald Spoto years later. "I was constantly falling in love, and it never occurred to me that this was wrong or bad."

Hitchcock considered Grace's style and beauty that were underscored by what he called her "sexual elegance" and wanted to make her the ultimate femme fatale of his suspenseful films. Hitchcock and Grace were to go on to make three films together and to develop a close friendship. In fact, Grace turned down the opportunity to co-star with Marlon Brando in *On the Waterfront* so that she could work with Hitchcock on *Rear Window*. Grace explained years later that she and Hitchcock discussed *Rear Window* frequently during *Dial M for Murder*. Grace's replacement in *On the Waterfront*, Eva Marie Saint, ended up winning an Academy Award for the role.

She often told interviewers that Alfred Hitchcock taught her everything she knew about cinema.

As *Rear Window* co-stars, Grace and Jimmy Stewart also developed a close friendship and one that by all accounts was a platonic one. In his role as L.B. Jeffries, a photographer who is laid up with a broken leg, Stewart calls Grace's character, Lisa Fremont "too perfect... She's too talented. She's too beautiful. She's too sophisticated. She's too everything but what I want."

The film, which opened in October 1954, earned Grace critical praise from reviewers such as the one from Variety who commented on the "earthy quality" of the relationship between Grace and Jimmy Stewart.

Grace's busy career next included a starring role opposite William Holden in *The Bridges at Toko-Ri*. After the film's release in January 1955, The New Yorker commented on the on-screen chemistry between Grace and Holden, and noted Grace's "quiet confidence." Next for Grace came her pivotal role as Georgie Elgin in the George Seaton film *The Country Girl*.

Bing Crosby, who was the male lead of the film, almost withdrew from the production when he discovered the identity of his young co-star, telling producers Grace was too inexperienced, too glamorous and too pretty for the role of Georgie.

Thanks to Grace's skill as an actress and Edith Head's skill as a costumer, Cosby changed his mind. Although the film's producers included flashback scenes that showed Kelly in her state of usual style perfection – they probably felt they had to -- Grace convincingly played the dowdy and neglected wife of an alcoholic.

Grace explained in an interview that she felt compelled to play a role that was more than just window dressing for the leading man's character, and she threw herself into preparations for the part.

Her director for *The Country Girl*, George Seaton said, "Some [actors] give you everything they've got at once and there it is – there is no more. But Grace is like a kaleidoscope: one twist and you get a whole new facet."

Grace's raw, honest, stripped-down performance earned her an Academy Award for Best Actress in 1954. Her acceptance speech was short and sweet:

"The thrill of this moment keeps me from saying what I really feel. I can only say thank you with all my heart to all who made this possible for me. Thank you!"

Apparently Judy Garland, who was the front runner for the Oscar that year, did not take the loss well. Reports say that an inebriated Garland, who was praised for her comeback performance in *A Star Is Born*, telephoned Grace later that night saying that Grace took away her last chance for a Best Actress Oscar, and that the award was rightfully hers before hanging up.

After the ceremony, according to Hollywood legend, Grace was spending the evening with Marlon Brando before they were interrupted by Bing Crosby. If you believe what you read, the two actors, who represented two very different types of leading men, had a shoving match about Grace.

The following year, 1955, Grace starred in the film *Green Fire* alongside Stewart Granger. Kelly played coffee plantation owner Catherine Knowland in the film, which was shot on location in Columbia and was a critical and box office flop. Grace later told Hedda Hopper that the filming experience, which included the crew getting shipwrecked, bad weather and living in a dirty hut – was extremely unpleasant.

Next up for Grace was perhaps her defining role as a glamorous young star in Alfred Hitchcock's *To Catch a Thief* with Cary Grant, who became a lifelong friend. Grant unabashedly named Grace as his favorite leading lady in an interview years later. "Well, with all due respect to dear Ingrid Bergman, I much preferred Grace. She had serenity."

Grant admired Grace for being friendly and open to everyone on the set, saying she had "no stuffy attitude, no star complex."

Grace's wardrobe was a sight to behold in *A Catch to Thief,* and she never looked lovelier. Filmed on location in the French Riviera, Hitchcock wanted the opulent location to be reflected in the clothing, and fashion designer Edith Head, who came to admire and develop a friendship with Grace, did not disappoint him with her costume designs. Among other costumes, Grace wears a ball gown complete with a golden crinoline skirt, a cerulean chiffon gown, a wide-brimmed sun hat and Capri pants, and even a stylish black swimsuit along with dark sun glasses.

Screenwriter John Michael Hayes had this to say about how Hitchcock felt about Grace: "Had he been able, Hitch would have used Grace in his next ten pictures. I would say that all the actresses he subsequently cast were attempts to retrieve the image and feeling that Hitch carried around so reverentially about Grace."

By this time, Grace may have already been tiring of the Hollywood scene and thinking about her future. She even admitted to a reporter that she would not want to marry someone who would feel inferior to her because of her fame and financial success.

After the filming for *To Catch a Thief* was complete in 1955, Grace flew back to America for the Oscars. She was asked to join the United States Delegation Committee at the Cannes Film Festival, so she was soon headed back to France. It was in Cannes at a planned photo shoot that she met her future husband, Prince Rainier of Monaco.

By the end of the year, the high-profile couple had announced their engagement. In fact, Grace wore her own engagement ring when she filmed her next film, *High Society*, a musical adaptation of *The Philadelphia Story*, with Bing Crosby and Frank Sinatra. Grace added another form of gold to her list of accolades for her duet with Bing Crosby in the song "True Love," which was written by Cole Porter. Although Grace only sings with crooner Bing Crosby on the final chorus, the hit song, released in 1956, went gold and then platinum, making it her first and only and Crosby's 21st gold record.

The final released film of Grace Kelly's whirlwind film career was *The Swan* with Alec Guiness. When the film was released in 1956, Grace received top billing for the only time of her brief but intensive career.

Coincidentally, Grace portrays a princess in the film. Her Princess Alexandra is a noblewoman in an un-named European country before the start of World War I who is torn between her feelings for a young royal tutor (Louis Jourdan) and the older, balding prince (Alec Guinness) to whom she is betrothed.

"Your whole life, your whole upbringing, has been devoted to just one thing: to make you fit to be a queen," Alexandra's mother tells her in the film. The film was shot at the 1895 Biltmore Estate of George W. Vanderbilt in Asheville and at Lake Junaluska in North Carolina.

In his biography of Grace, Donald Spoto refers to a note Alec Guinness wrote to his wife while he was filming *The Swan* with Louis Jourdan. The note says that, despite spending an entire evening gossiping about Grace, Guiness, Jourdan and Jourdan's wife only were able to agree on the fact that Grace was an enigma.

Even though filming for *The Swan* ended in December 1955, in order to capitalize on all the hoopla that came to surround Grace's nuptials, MGM held the release of *The Swan* to coincide with the wedding day of Grace and her real-life prince on April 19, 1956.

Chapter 3: Marriage

Opinions differed – and still do – as to whether Grace's marriage to Prince Rainier III of Monaco was the result of a fairytale romance or a business arrangement.

At the time of her engagement, Grace, age 26, was one of the highest paid and most respected actresses in the world, and she had been romantically linked with many of Hollywood's leading men. Prince Rainier, 32, was the ruling monarch of the tiny principality of Monaco and was rumored to be shopping for a bride.

Prince Rainier headed the House of Grimaldi, Europe's longest-ruling princely family which had reigned continuously since 1297. Though Rainier's domain was just 370 acres, including a 200-room pink palace and a private zoo, Monaco included the famed but somewhat fading Monte Carlo Casino, which provided enough revenue that none of Rainier's 20,000 subjects had to pay personal income tax. Under the terms of a 1918 treaty with France, however, if Rainier did not produce an heir, Monaco would revert to French control. After a lengthy relationship with French actress Gisèle Pascal ended (ironically in part because of her affair with Gary Cooper and because of her desire to continue her acting career) Prince Rainier, it seemed, needed to get married.

Despite her many romantic relationships, Grace was only engaged once before she met Rainier, and it appeared to have been a bit of a loose arrangement at that. She had a two year on-again, off-again relationship with Russian dress designer Oleg Cassini, who later gained international fame as the designer for First Lady Jackie Kennedy.

Cassini, who was divorced from actress Gene Tierney, said in a 1983 article about Grace in People Magazine, "I fell in love with Grace after I saw her in *Mogambo*. When she broke up with Milland she sent me a postcard asking me to come to the south of France while she filmed *To Catch a Thief*. 'Those who love me follow me,' she wrote."

Cassini apparently was eager to oblige and devoted himself to Grace. For a time, Grace ignored her family's objections that Cassini was both too old for her, had too much of a temper and was inappropriate for her because he was divorced. Cassini maintained the couple was secretly engaged.

Grace was seeing an old flame, actor Jean-Pierre Aumont, in fact, when she met Rainier in 1955 at a photo session at the Cannes Film Festival. Aumont later told reporters that Grace almost missed the photo shoot because it conflicted with an appointment to have her hair done, explaining that he advised her: "You can't possibly do that! He's a reigning prince."

Later, Aumont said Grace told him that she found the prince "very charming." After their meeting, which seemed casual enough at the time, Grace and the prince began a private correspondence, which was encouraged by Father Francis Tucker, an American priest who served as Rainier's closest aide.

Prince Rainier later explained that with each letter, he and Grace "revealed more and more about each other." He admits to Donald Spoto in the book *High Society: The Life of Grace Kelly* that it had been difficult for him to find someone who could be a soul mate as well as a lover. In their many letters back and forth, Rainier said the couple had the opportunity to become pen pals and then close friends "long before they ever held hands."

Grace's friend Rita Gam told People Magazine, "I remember her saying, 'I found my prince.' I thought she meant the generic term. Then I found out he really was a prince."

On his way to the United States for a visit several months later, Rainier mysteriously described his future wife as someone with hair "the color of autumn leaves. Her eyes are blue or violet, with flecks of gold."

At a press conference after he arrived in New York, reporters asked Rainier directly if he was there in search of a wife. After replying "No" to that question, the follow-up question was: "If you were pursuing a wife, what kind would you like?" Rainier smiled before answering: "I don't know – the best."

Several days later, Prince Rainier met with Grace and her family. Her outspoken father, Jack, reportedly told the prince before giving his consent that royalty meant nothing to him and that he hoped he would not "run around" or else he was sure to lose "a mighty fine girl."

Ever mindful of the need for him to produce an heir, Rainier reportedly took a doctor with him to test Grace's ability to bear children. Thinking the doctor wanted to test her virginity, Grace refused at first.

Three days later, Rainier proposed, giving Grace a friendship band with diamonds and rubies, until her real engagement ring, a breathtaking Cartier design that featured a 10.47-carat emerald-cut diamond and two baguette diamonds mounted in platinum, could be made.

After their engagement was made public, Grace gushed to her friend Rita Gam, "I love his eyes. I could look into them for hours."

As preparations began for what was to be called the "wedding of the century," rumors swirled about the financial aspects of the marriage. Some magazines reported that the Kelly family was providing Prince Rainier with a dowry of $2 million, and other fan magazines bemoaned what looked to be the end of Grace's flourishing film career.

When asked for his reaction to the engagement, Alfred Hitchcock quipped to a newspaper reporter that he was happy that Grace Kelly "has found herself such a good part."

By the time Grace met her prince, she appeared to be destined to marry someone of a huge celebrity status. She had even told a reporter that she never wanted to hear a restaurant maître d' refer to her spouse as Mr. Kelly. On the other side of the equation, Rainier would do well to bring Grace's glamour and elegance as well as the sense of Hollywood excitement that would follow her to his then somewhat sleepy small kingdom.

In order for her to officially become Her Serene Highness Princess Gracia Patricia of Monaco, Grace and Rainier needed to have two wedding ceremonies: a civil ceremony, which was set for April 18, and a Roman Catholic Church wedding, which was to follow on April 19. From the time the dates were set in January 1956, Grace's wedding, which she privately called, "the circus of the century" was hardly ever out of the news. Biographer Robert Lacey calls it "the first modern event to generate media overkill."

Grace, who by this time was used to being hounded by photographers, was followed everywhere she went. Life Magazine did a full spread of photographs showing Grace shopping for her trousseau and for a gift for her groom. In Monaco, workers busily painted and redecorated the royal palace.

The preparations culminated with Grace, her family, her black poodle and her more than 80 pieces of luggage taking an eight-day ocean voyage from Pier 84 in New York Harbor aboard the ocean liner SS Constitution for the French Riviera. Those 80 suitcases included a dozen of the dresses Helen Rose designed for Grace for the film *High Society*, which were a gift to the bride from MGM, as well as a trousseau of some 40 outfits she purchased during that pre-nuptial shopping trip in New York City. The color palette of her new wardrobe included beige, soft pastels and her favorite color, yellow.

Although nearly 400 reporters applied to sail on the journey, most of them were turned away. Howell Conant was the only photographer allowed to take pictures of the princess-to-be on the voyage. Thousands of fans, however, lined the dock, many of them armed with flowers and cameras, to wish the Kelly entourage a bon voyage. Across the ocean, more than 20,000 people lined the streets to greet the princess in Monaco when she arrived.

The 40 minute civil ceremony was held in the baroque throne room in the Palace of Monaco and was attended by only 80 close family members and friends. Grace wore a light pink dress made of taffeta and accented with cream Alençon lace, along with white kid gloves and a Juliet cap. Rainier wore traditional formal wear of a white vest, gray tie, striped trousers and a black morning coat. After exchanging their vows in French, which was required by law, the new husband and wife stepped out onto the palace balcony to wave to the hundreds of onlookers waiting below.

That evening, the couple hosted a public reception for the citizens of Monaco, so that each one could meet and shake hands with the new princess. A large celebration took place at the Opera House later that evening.

The following morning, at 9:30 a.m. on April 19, 1956, 600 invited guests filled St. Nicholas Cathedral to witness the religious wedding ceremony at a high mass celebrated by the Bishop of Monaco. An estimated 30 million people watched the event live on television. Hydrangeas, white lilacs, lilies, and snapdragons decorated the altar and the church.

Grace's sister, Peggy, served as matron of honor. Her six bridesmaids wore yellow silk organdy dresses designed by Joe Allen Hong at Neiman Marcus after Lawrence Marcus visited Monaco. Grace's six junior attendants, including four girls and two boys, were dressed in white.

As a gift to the bride, MGM Studios gave costume designer Helen Rose, who had dressed her in *High Society* and *The Swan*, the task of designing Grace's real-life fairy tale wedding gown. Paramount's Edith Head, who designed the fabulous blue satin gown Grace wore when she accepted her Oscar, designed Grace's going-away suit.

Along with about three dozen seamstresses, Rose worked on the spectacular wedding gown for six weeks. The white dress featured a high collar, long sleeves, a fitted bodice and a voluminous skirt made of silk taffeta, tulle and century-old Brussels rose point lace. Newspaper columnists' comments on the dress ranged from "serenely regal," to a "charming dress though not a superb one" to "magnificent." The New York Times called it "the loveliest example of the American product." Another reporter described the long train as "flowing like a river of whipped cream among the plush red floor."

Under her wedding gown, Grace's petticoats were covered with tiny blue satin bows. For Grace's head, Rose designed a Juliet cap that was decorated with orange blossoms and a 90-yard-long veil. MGM's chief hairstylist Sydney

Guilaroff, styled Grace's hair in an elegant upsweep for her wedding.

Grace carried a small Bible with an embroidered white cover and a bridal bouquet of lilies of the valley. Prince Rainier wore a Napoleonic military uniform he designed himself for the wedding. The bride and groom did not look at each other during the ceremony, but sat, stood and knelt facing the high altar as instructed by Monsignor Marella, the Papal Legate from Paris.

The wedding guest list included Hollywood stars Cary Grant, David Niven, Gloria Swanson and Ava Gardner as well as many heads of state and diplomats. At the wedding reception, the people of Monaco gave the royal newlyweds a cream and black Rolls-Royce convertible, and they sliced the six-tier wedding cake together with the prince's sword.

Grace and Rainier left Monaco that night for a seven-week Mediterranean honeymoon cruise with planned stops in Spain and Corsica. Grace was reportedly frequently quite seasick on the trip.

Still thought to be one of the most beautiful wedding ceremonies of all time, Grace's wedding was filmed and later released as

America as "Wedding in Monaco." The filming was part of an agreement Grace made agreement with MGM as a release from her unfulfilled contract with the studio. Grace later gave her gown, cap, veil, shoes and prayer book to the Philadelphia Museum of Art.

As one of the most beautiful and most photographed women in the world, Grace was often asked how she could leave Hollywood at the height of her film career. "When I married Prince Rainier, I married the man and not what he represented or what he was," she said later. "I fell in love with him without giving a thought to anything else."

Much has been written about Grace and her prince and their relationship. Some biographers say they were devoted to each other. Some say he had affairs from the beginning of their marriage; others say that, eventually, they both looked for love outside the marriage.

In an ABC television interview, Grace herself admitted that the idea of her life as a fairy tale was in itself a fairy tale.

Chapter 4: Princess of Monaco

After her wedding, Grace Kelly abandoned her acting career in order to become Princess Consort of Monaco, and Prince Rainier banned her films from being shown in Monaco. Her new royal position also required her to give up her United States citizenship.

Grace later said it was difficult for her to try to become a normal person –as if being a princess is a normal person -- after having been a movie star for so long. She did succeed in bringing her youth and American viewpoint to Monaco, including banning the long-standing law that anyone calling her had to be female, and the requirement any woman calling upon her had to wear a hat.

Despite all the changes and challenges of her new life, Grace spoke very kindly of her prince. She said in an interview not long after her marriage that Rainier was bright, warm, handsome and that he could make her giggle.

It turned out that Grace had little to adjust to being "just" a princess. She soon had another role to take on – that of being a mother. Just nine months and four days after the wedding, January 23, 1957, Grace gave birth to Princess Caroline, the first of her and Prince Rainier's three children. On the day of Caroline's birth, 21 guns announced the news while a national holiday was called and all gambling ceased in Monaco.

Just over a year later 101 guns announced the birth of the couple's son, Prince Albert, on March 14, 1958. The birth of Princess Stéphanie completed the family of five on February 1, 1965.

Grace clearly enjoyed being a mother and she looks her most relaxed in candid photos of her with her children. Photographer Howell Conant, whose famous photographs of Grace include the striking ones he took of her rising from the water with wet hair in Jamaica in 1955, and who became a close friend of Grace, said, "I loved photographing Grace when she was with her children, if only because she could get so involved with them that she paid little attention to me and my camera."

Conant was the only photographer allowed to get close to the princess-to-be on her 1956 voyage to Monaco, and he became unofficial photographer to the House of Grimaldi, extensively photographing Grace, her husband and their children. He later said of the Jamaica shots, which were so uncharacteristic of the photos of movie stars of the day, "You trusted Grace's beauty...You knew it wasn't built from clothes and makeup...this was Grace: natural, unpretentious."

Contrary to tradition, Grace took care of many of her little ones' needs herself. "The nursery doors were open, and the children were very much a part of the fabric of the day," recalled her close friend, Rita Gam.

Grace tried to give her children as much of a normal upbringing as possible, but they did live in a fish bowl. She frequently brought her children to visit family in Philadelphia, and Prince Albert attended a camp for several summers with his American cousins.

"The sometimes inquisitive and unhealthy interest that the media show in us is often the source of childish anxieties that are hard to allay," Grace admitted. "I do everything I can to protect my children from them."

In addition to raising her children, Grace spent her time managing charities and administering some of Monaco's cultural affairs. She told reporters that her experience in the limelight as an actress helped make her in her new position and that she felt she had a natural inclination to feel compassion for her subjects and their concerns.

By the early 1960s, Grace may have felt some of the constraints of palace life. Photographer Eve Arnold, who visited Monaco in 1962 to work on a CBS documentary, said she got the feeling that Grace felt trapped in her life as a princess and that the life she witnessed was far from the fairy tale she had expected.

When her mentor Alfred Hitchcock offered her the lead in his film *Marnie,* Grace was excited to accept. And when it was determined that all the filming could take place during a Grimaldi family vacation to the States, Prince Rainier agreed to his wife taking the role.

"There have been times when the princess has been a little melancholic – which I quite understand – about having performed a form of art very successfully, only to be shut away from it completely," Rainier told biographer Peter Hawkins in 1966.

An official palace press release dated March 19, 1962 announced that "Princess Grace has accepted to appear during her summer vacation in a motion picture for Mr. Alfred Hitchcock, to be made in the United States." To allay any concerns about the Princess returning to Monaco, the release went on to say that Grace would return to Monaco with her family in November.

No one was prepared for the uproar that followed this official announcement. Newspapers were filled with commentary that ranged from saying Grace was returning to Hollywood to raise money for her husband's troubled kingdom, to that the move was a pointed snub to French General Charles de Gaulle to prove Monaco's independence from France, to the rumor that Grace and Rainier were having serious marital troubles. MGM added a legal concern to the fray, saying that if Grace returned to acting it should be to work for MGM, as she had an unfulfilled contract with the studio.

In an effort to ease concerns among Monaco's citizenry, the Palace announced that Grace's salary for the film role, speculated to be close to $1 million, would go to a special foundation for deprived children and young athletes in Monaco.

The uproar worsened, however, and in June 1962, Grace, who had initially "bubbled like a teenager" about the role, according to her friend Judy Kanter, resolutely told reporters that she was not going to make the Hitchcock movie after all.

She wrote in a letter to Alfred Hitchcock dated June 18, 1962: "I was so excited about doing it, and particularly about working with you again. When we meet I would like to explain to you myself all of the reasons, which would be difficult to do in a letter or through a third party. It is unfortunate that it had to happen this way, and I am deeply sorry."

After writing a letter back to Grace that included the phrase "It's only a movie," one of his favorite expressions, a disappointed Hitchcock offered the role to actress Tippi Hedren.

Although bitterly disappointed, Grace tried to throw herself into her duties as princess. In 1963, she helped to establish AMADE, a humanitarian non-profit group also called The World Association of Children's Friends to promote and protect the "moral and physical integrity" and "spiritual well-being of children throughout the world, without distinction of race, nationality or religion and in a spirit of complete political independence."

Grace served as president for Monaco's chapter of the Red Cross and brought many of her Hollywood friends, including Frank Sinatra and Cary Grant, to Monaco for Red Cross fundraisers. In 1959, Grace was given a medal of merit by the Austrian government for Monaco's Red Cross aid to Hungarian refugees who were fleeing Russian invasion.

Each year, Grace organized and hosted a Christmas party with personalized gifts for all the children in Monaco's orphanage. She also became active in La Leche League, the international organization founded in the United States that encourages breastfeeding. She served as president of the Garden Club of Monaco, and as president of the organizing committee of the International Arts Foundation. She was most proud of the Princess Grace Foundation, which she established in 1964 to encourage young people in the creative arts, and to provide arts scholarships for eligible students.

In September 1958, Monaco's hospital was renamed The Princess Grace Hospital Center in honor of Grace's humanitarian projects. The princess was a frequent visitor to new mothers in the hospital's maternity ward, and to the young patients in the children's ward.

Grace also enjoyed surprising residents of Monaco's retirement homes with unexpected visits. She was also responsible for Monaco's first day care center opening in 1966. She often visited the center armed with toys and books.

In 1966 Grace started the International Monte Carlo Ballet Festival, today called the Spring Arts Festival. In 1968, she was also responsible for the founding of the Monaco Garden Club, which runs an annual international floral competition.

Although Grace lived with her husband and children in the 200-room palace, the family maintained a private retreat just across the border in France at Roc Agel. Grace also went home to the United States for visits on a regular basis. As her children grew, she enjoyed being involved in their education and activities.

In an interview with Plain Truth Magazine for a March 1974 issue that focused upon royalty and family values, Grace said, "What better 'thing' of one's own can one do than share in the creation of a new life, thereafter integrating it into a loving and wholesome family and continuing to guide the formation of its personality and the molding of its character?"

Although she certainly missed certain aspects of her acting career, she often spoke of the problems in film industry. "Hollywood amuses me," she once admitted, calling the film capital "holier-than-thou for the public and unholier-than-the-devil in reality."

Chapter 5: Later years

In her 26 years as princess, Grace was responsible for renewing energy and interest in the principality that became her adopted home. Louissette Levy-Soussan Azzoaglio, her secretary of 19 years said in a People Magazine interview that Grace had been a professional actress and that she had been a professional princess. "The princess polished up Monaco's image from the moment she arrived," Azzoaglio said.

By the late 1970s, however, with two children out of the home and her youngest, Stéphanie, a teenager, Grace was ready to broaden her horizons. She began dividing her time among the palace in Monaco; Roc Agel, the family's hilltop farm across the border in France; and a townhouse in Paris, as she looked for more artistic pursuits to take up her time.

She took her life-long interest in flowers to a new level with dried floral arranging. She even had some of her pieces displayed in a Paris gallery and sold a few of them, donating any proceeds to charity. Grace's *My Book of Flowers*, published in 1980, is a comprehensive work about the flowers and plants of Monaco, as well as Monaco's floral traditions and legends.

After the Marnie fiasco, Grace resisted attempts to do another film, including repeated requests by director Herbert Ross to have her participate in his 1977 film, *The Turning Point*. When asked about returning to the screen, Grace usually said that she simply did not have the time needed to devote to it.

Grace did lend her voice to the narration of a few documentary films, including *Children of Theater Street*, a film about the Kirov Ballet School in Leningrad, and ABC's made-for-television film *The Poppy Is Also a Flower* in 1966.

In 1976, the former MGM actress joined the board of directors of Twentieth Century-Fox Film Corporation. She also was responsible for the restoration of a theater in Monte Carlo which was renamed the Théâtre Princesse Grace.

Beginning in 1976, Grace conducted a poetry reading tour in Europe and America, donating all proceeds to her non-profit Princess Grace Foundation. In honor of America's bicentennial celebration, Grace selected some poems that she felt illustrated the American spirit to read at the Edinburgh Festival. When she received both critical and audience acclaim for her readings, Grace was both surprised and delighted. She seemed to be finding a way to combine her love of the spoken word and of drama with her ongoing role as a dignified princess.

"The poetry reading is something that doesn't take too much time, and that I can do occasionally," she explained in an interview. "For the most part I do it for students or for people interested in poetry. I get a lot of satisfaction from it."

At the time of her death, she had poetry readings scheduled in California, at UCLA, and in Palm Springs. She also was working on a film project called *Rearranged* in which she played herself. It was never completed.

Some of Grace's friends and former colleagues believed she would have returned to acting on a part-time basis. "She missed acting because she wasn't challenged enough in other ways," her friend Rita Gam said. "There was a black hole in her life."

Grace's modest wood-paneled den in the palace reflected her sense of humor and her previous life. Amongst stickers and plaques reading "In God we trust, all others pay cash" and "We'd love to help you out, which way did you come in?" she kept her gold record for *True Love* and her Oscar for *The Country Girl.*

During her marriage, Grace had several miscarriages but biographer Donald Spoto said she was able to maintain a "poised facade" despite her sadness and disappointments.

"I certainly don't think of my life as a fairy tale," she said in an ABC television interview in 1980. "I think of myself as a modern, contemporary woman who has had to deal with all kinds of problems that many women today have to deal with. I am still coping—trying to cope."

When asked if she had considered writing a memoir, Grace admitted that she had never kept personal journals. The dutiful daughter, who was always trying to please her father, Jack, even after he died, replied that she was thinking of writing one about Jack Kelly.

She also told People Magazine that she was looking forward to seeing her three children happily married and to being a grandmother.

As one of the world's most beautiful women, Grace was asked how she felt about aging gracefully. "No one likes the idea of getting older," she said in the ABC interview a few years before she died. "It's a question of facing the inevitable and not getting upset about it."

Grace's family:

Shortly after Grace's marriage, her father, Jack, died. His hometown of Philadelphia erected a prominent statue of the Olympic champion near the finish line of the Schuylkill River course where he once competed. It is located just off of the scenic "Kelly Drive," which is named for Grace's brother, Kell (Jack Jr.)

After the death of her husband, Grace's mother moved out of the family home and into an apartment in the Alden Park Towers around the corner. She suffered a stroke in 1975 and was never told of her daughter's death. "It's fortunate she doesn't know," Lizanne said in a 1983 interview. "We have endured the pain of Grace's passing for her."

Grace's sister Peggy, always her father's favorite, had two unsuccessful marriages before dying, presumed to be from the ravages of alcoholism, at the age of 65 in 1991. She had two daughters.

Grace's brother, Kell (John B. Kelly, Jr.) rowed in single scull competition in the 1948 Summer Olympics in London, the 1952 Summer Olympics in Helsinki and the 1956 Summer Olympics in Melbourne. He participated in the double scull at the 1960 Olympics in Rome. Kell won a bronze medal at the 1956 Games and also won the gold medal at the 1955 Pan American Games in Mexico City. Kell left his wife Mary, a former Olympic swimmer, and their six children to live with Rachel Harlow, who, interestingly enough, was the former Richard Finocchio who went through a sex-change operation.

The well-publicized relationship was a factor in Kell's decision to drop out of the 1975 mayoral contest in Philadelphia when his opponent threatened to campaign with the slogan "Do you want Rachel Harlow as First Lady of Philadelphia?"

Kell died at age 57 of a massive heart attack he suffered while jogging along East River Drive (now Kelly Drive) near Boathouse Row along the Schuylkill River in Philadelphia after his customary morning row. He and his second wife, Sandra, a banker, did not have any children.

Grace's younger sister, Lizanne, and her husband, Donald LeVine, had two children, including a daughter she named after her famous sister. Ironically, Donald died of a heart attack within an hour of Kell's heart attack in 1985. Lizanne continued to live in the big house at 26th Street and Wesley Avenue in Ocean City, N.J. that Jack Kelly built for his family in 1929. It stayed in the Kelly family for 72 years before Lizanne sold it in 2001. Lizanne died in 2009 in a retirement community outside of Philadelphia.

Lizanne reflected on how Grace's becoming a princess affected her privacy in a 2008 interview. She recalled how fans would climb or hang over the wall, looking in the family's vacation home windows, but that Ocean City residents were respectful of the family privacy.

In the interview, Lizanne mentioned that the year 1982 was the first time her sister Grace missed the family's annual Labor Day barbecue and beach party at Ocean City. When Lizanne sold the Spanish Mission Revival style her father Jack built as a summer getaway for his family, she was the last of her siblings to survive.

After battling coronary problems and lung infections for several years, Prince Rainier died on April 6, 2005 at the age of 81. Although he was rumored to be involved with other women, he never remarried. When asked about remarriage, he told his biographer Jeffrey Robinson, "How could I? Everywhere I go, I see Grace."

According to Robinson, a part of Rainier died with Grace. He said that although the Prince kept his sense of humor, there was a sense of loneliness and melancholy in him after Grace's death. Rainier was buried next to Grace in the Grimaldi family vault in St. Nicholas Cathedral.

Princess Caroline married investment banker and playboy Philippe Junot in 1978, but divorced him two years later. In 1983, Caroline married Italian businessman Stefano Casiraghi, but she was tragically widowed when Casiraghi lost control of his powerboat in a race and it came down on top of him. Andrea Albert Pierre Casiraghi, who was born in 1984, is her eldest child and is second in line to the throne of Monaco after his mother. Caroline's third husband and the father of four of her children is Ernst August V, Prince of Hanover, the head of the House of Hanover.

According to Wendy Leigh in her book *True Grace: The Life and Times of an American Princess*, Grace tried unsuccessfully to make a match between Caroline and England's Prince Charles. Grace's nephew, Christian de Massy, told Leigh that Grace got along very well with Prince Charles and liked the British royal family.

Grace's son, Albert, is Prince of Monaco, the head of the House of Grimaldi and the current ruler of the Principality of Monaco. Since Albert's two children, Jazmin Grace Grimaldi and Alexandre Coste, were born out of wedlock, they are not in line for the throne. He married former South African swimmer Charlene Wittstock in 2011. Like Grace, the mother-in-law she never knew, Princess Charlene is known for her elegant sense of style.

Princess Stéphanie is currently the seventh in the line of succession to the Monegasque throne. She has been a singer, a swimwear designer and a fashion model. She has two children from her marriage to her bodyguard Daniel Ducruet: Louis Robert Paul Ducruet and Pauline Grace Magui Ducruet. The couple divorced in 1996. Stéphanie gave birth to her third child, Camille Marie Kelly Gottlieb, in 1998. As her parents were not married, she is not in the line of succession to the Monégasque throne. Stéphanie married Portuguese acrobat Adans Lopez Peres in 2003 and divorced him in 2004.

Chapter 6: Death

Princess Grace began to suffer from severe headaches and high blood pressure in 1982. On September 13, 1982, Grace and 17-year-old Stéphanie were returning to Monaco from Roc-Agel, the family's country estate on the French side of the border.

All that week, Grace and Stephanie had been discussing whether Stéphanie would attend the prestigious Institute of Fashion Design in Paris or, as Stephanie desired, race-car driving school with her then-boyfriend, Paul Belmondo.

Perhaps to give her more time to talk with her daughter, Grace assured her chauffeur that she would be fine driving herself and took the wheel of her brown Land Rover 3500 herself for the 35-minute drive back to Monaco. Ten minutes into the trip, however, as she was driving down the narrow winding road, Grace momentarily lost consciousness. When she came to, authorities think she may have pressed the accelerator instead of the brake. No skid marks were found later on the road. Stéphanie recalled later that her mother said she could not stop the car. Stéphanie reached over to out the car into park, but it was not enough to stop the vehicle from heading over the edge of the road and down a 120-foot embankment.

Contrary to legend, the accident was not at the same spot where Grace's character worried Cary Grant's character in *To Catch a Thief*, although the roads do look similar. Grace's Rover struck a tree and rolled onto a pile of rocks, crushing both the passenger-side door and roof. Neither Grace nor Stéphanie was wearing a seatbelt.

A motorist driving behind the Rover reported to police that the car in front of him was swerving erratically back and forth, and he honked his horn a few times to get the attention of what he assumed was a drunk or sleepy driver. He estimated that as Grace's car approached the hairpin curve known as "Devil's Curse," it accelerated suddenly to 50 m.p.h. or more before crashing through the stone barrier and heading down the 120-foot hillside.

Grace and Stéphanie were taken to the hospital in Monaco (later renamed the Princess Grace Hospital Center), but at the time the facility was not well equipped for brain injuries.

Doctors performed surgery to stop Grace's internal bleeding, but her other injuries included multiple fractures of the collar bone, thigh and ribs. When it was determined that a local doctor had the necessary CAT scan equipment to diagnose her head injuries, doctors decided to move the princess there for the test. The decision to move Grace for the test has since been scrutinized as possible exacerbating her head injuries.

When doctors told the family the next day that Grace would never recover, the Prince and his children made the agonizing decision to remove her from life support. Grace Kelly died on September 14, 1982. She was 52.

Doctors later said that a CAT scan showed Grace had suffered a mild cerebral hemorrhage before the accident. Her death was caused by a second hemorrhage, probably caused by the trauma of accident.

The body of Princess Grace would lie in state in an open coffin until September 18, when funeral services were held at the Cathedral of St. Nicholas in Monaco, the same church where Grace and Rainier were married in 1956. Four hundred people attended the funeral service including First Lady Nancy Reagan, Diana, Princess of Wales and Cary Grant, who wept through the entire service. Princess Stephanie, whose injuries prevented her from attending her mother's funeral, was too emotional to watch the televised service from her hospital bed.

Grace was buried in the Grimaldi family vault in the Cathedral. Prince Rainier, who never remarried, was buried alongside her following his death in 2005. Her marble slab is inscribed with the words (translated from the Latin): Grace Patricia, wife of Prince Rainier III, died the year of our Lord, 1982.

The family received tens of thousands of letters and cards of condolence, and mourners continued to leave flowers at the site of the crash accident for months after the accident. A few days after the crash, the car was crushed, taken out to sea and dropped there. When he was criticized for moving the car before it was fully examined for evidence, Rainier said it was to prevent people from taking piece of the vehicle as macabre souvenirs.

Prince Rainier admitted to writer Roger Bianchini that he had "a heaviness of heart that I don't think will change in my lifetime."

Caroline told Jeffrey Robinson for his 1989 book *Rainier and Grace: An Intimate Portrait* that her mother had not been feeling well that whole summer of 1982. ``She was incredibly tired. She never mentioned it or complained about it, though. But she wasn't in great form.''

A gardener who heard the car crash told numerous reporters that he pulled Stéphanie out of the driver`s side window, which gave the impression Stéphanie had been driving. She explained to Robinson that she lost consciousness as the car fell down the embankment. She said she remembered the car hitting a tree and the next thing she recalled was seeing smoke coming out of the car and thinking the car was going to explode.

After pushing the car door out with her legs, Stéphanie was able to get out of the car and yell to a woman who had arrived on the scene, " Please get help, call the palace, I`m Princess Stéphanie, call my father and get help." She told Robinson that other details were blurred until police arrived.

Eerily, Grace may have predicted how she would die. According to the book *True Grace: The Life And Times Of An American Princess* by Wendy Leigh, Grace once said to psychic Frank Andrews: "I've always had a premonition that I'm going to die in a car crash. Will I?"

French investigators ruled out a mechanical failure and concluded that the accident occurred when Grace blacked out and lost control of the car.

Rumors ran rampant, including various conspiracy theories. "They (the media) did their best to keep the story running and didn`t show much human compassion for the pain that we were suffering," Rainier told Robinson.

Despite palace efforts to shield her from it, the media's scrutiny and pressure on young Princess Stephanie was enormous. Stephanie told Robinson that because of all the "magic" surrounding her mother's life that is was hard for her fans to accept that Grace could do something as mortal as have a car accident. "People figured I must have caused it because she was too perfect to do something like that," Stephanie told Robinson.

Friends and family members reported that Prince Rainier always seemed a bit lost after Grace's death. He shared his feelings about his loss in a 1983 Associated Press in interview. He mentioned that Grace was good at being by his side as a partner, adding sadly "We worked as a team and the team has been split up."

Chapter 7: Legacy

Famous people are often asked about what they would like to leave behind, and Grace was no exception. Long before her untimely death, she remarked in a television interview that she would like to be remembered as someone who was a kind and loving person. "I would like to leave the memory of a human being with a correct attitude and who did her best to help others," she added.

On October 28, 2013, Grace's son Albert, now Prince Albert of Monaco and his elegant wife Princess Charlene of Monaco attended the opening of an retrospective exhibit "Grace Kelly: Behind the Icon" at the Michener Art Museum in Philadelphia. On view were personal photos, love letters to Grace from Prince Rainier, her Oscar for best actress, film clips, home movies and some of her famous dresses and accessories.

In a video recorded introduction for the exhibit, Albert referred to "my beautiful mother" and spoke of Grace's warm parenting style. The prince said he admired her passion for helping underprivileged children and in finding and rewarding creative talent in young people.

After leaving a successful Hollywood career to pursue her heart, Albert said Grace became an international spokesperson for arts and culture and established a legacy to help others through the Monaco Red Cross and through her Princess Grace Foundation.

"Those of us who were fortunate enough to know my mother, her family and friends, knew her to be a genuine, warm and loving woman: a woman who always put her family first."

At an event unveiling details of the exhibit in August 2013, held appropriately enough at the Hotel Monaco in downtown Philadelphia, Grace's nephew Christopher LeVine remembered his aunt fondly, describing how he once saw her packing up ingredients for Philadelphia scrapple – a loaf of pork scraps and cornmeal – to bring back to Monaco so the palace chef could re-create the dish she loved.

"She was going to tell him that it was a certain special paté from Philadelphia," Le Vine told an appreciative audience at the event. "She had her Philadelphia roots with her wherever she went."

Grace Kelly was in the public eye for most of her life. Her beauty, elegance and poise captured the world's attention both in her films and in her work as a princess. A veteran of newspaper rumors and gossip, Grace quipped in her later years, "The freedom of the press works in such a way that there is not much freedom from it."

Grace became a style icon, and her sense of style is essential part of anyone studying fashion of the 1950s. People Magazine listed Grace on its Best Dressed List of All Time in 2000, noting that she "embodied High Society with her white gloves, nipped-in jackets and crisp ball gowns. "

When Grace used a distinctive Hermès bag to conceal her first pregnancy from photographers, the purse became an enduring piece of fashion history, so much so that Hermès changed the name of the bag – introduced in 1935 as Sac à dépêches – to the Kelly Bag.

The Kelly Bag comes in five different sizes and is easily identifiable by its metal-tipped clasp, which can be closed with a tiny padlock. The key usually dangles from the handle of the leather purse, which has been an enduring fashion status symbol of the past half century.

Grace had her sense of fashion from an early age. Since her mother, Margaret, never approved of what she called "frippery," Grace favored classic styles. Her standard audition outfit in the late 1940s and early 1950s included white gloves, neutral hose, low-heeled shoes, slim wool skirts, camel-hair coat, a pair of horn-rimmed glasses (Grace was near-sighted) and very little makeup.

Grace's friend Rita Gam described Grace's style as that of a "small-town high-school teacher." Fashion Designer Oleg Cassini, called it her "Bryn Mawr look." Her one-time fiancée also pointed out that Grace's style was based in the fact that she always dressed like a lady.

Grace's sense of sense of style endures today and is having a lasting influence.

Referring to the pastel colors, beautiful luxury fabrics and feminine necklines of the 1950s, fashion historian June Weir wrote that Grace had the perfect beauty for that decade. Jenny Lister, Curator of 19th Century Textiles and Fashion at the Victoria and Albert Museum, noted that Grace had a polished and well-accessorized look that is classic, elegant and practical at the same time.

That ambiguous, too good to be true "look" that Grace could pull off so well was one of the reasons Alfred Hitchcock wanted Grace in his films and is one of the main reasons why her on-screen presence still captivates audiences who view her films today.

Other than the good genes she inherited from her parents, what were some of Grace's beauty secrets?

Gina McKinnon, author of the 2013 book *What Would Grace Do?*, tells Allure.com: "It sounds really basic, but she looked after herself — she drank lots of water, she didn't smoke, she swam a lot, and when she was younger she did ballet."

Grace studied ballet until a teacher told her when she was a teenager that she was too tall to make it as a ballerina. The rigorous training served her well. Her erect posture and her way of almost gliding through a room – especially noticeable in her scenes in the apartment in the film *Rear Window* -- added to her graceful image.

Grace's minimalist use of make-up was also influential. At a time when many actresses used heavier colors, Grace usually selected neutral shades, often adding a light tawny brown eye shadow along her eyebrows and using two shades of blusher - a lighter tone over the bone, and a darker shade in the hollows to help define her cheekbones.

Grace said she learned important information about how to make herself appear well on camera during her early career as a model. One of the lessons she learned was that she looked best with her hair pulled back off her face. It was a look few could – or can -- pull off, and it made her seem all the more striking. Calling herself loyal to her old clothes, Grace also inherently knew what styles worked to accentuate her tiny waist and regal posture.

In October 2009, a plaque was placed on the "Rodeo Drive Walk of Style" in recognition of Princess Grace's contributions to style and fashion. The beautiful 2011 wedding dress of Catherine, Duchess of Cambridge ("Kate" Middleton) was inspired by Grace's 1956 dress. The silk gown with spaghetti straps that Grace wore to accept her Oscar for Best Actress for *The Country Girl* cost $4,000 and was the most expensive Oscar gown to date.

Howell Conant, the trusted Grimaldi family photographer who captured the youthful Grace so beautifully in those natural photos in Jamaica, published *Grace: An Intimate Portrait of Princess Grace* by Her Friend and Favorite Photographer in 1992. The book contains photographs, including many candid shots that capture her warmth as a woman, and as a wife and mother.

Grace's image has found its way into many aspects of our culture. In 1993, for example, she became the first American actress to appear on a U.S. postage stamp. She is referenced in several popular songs, including "Grace Kelly with Wings" by Piebald, "Grace Kelly" by Mika, "Grace Kelly" by the Motion Sick, "Grace Kelly Blues" by Eels, ""We Didn't Start the Fire" by Billy Joel, "Vogue" by Madonna, "Grace Kelly" by Los Coquillos, "'59" by Brian Setzer Orchestra, "Six Billion People" by Paul Gilbert, "Four Flights Up" by Lloyd Cole and the Commotions, "That Night" by Rufus Wainwright, "Bend Over, I'll Drive" by The Cramps "Grace Kelly" by Die Ärzte" and "Princess Grace" by Spuds.

In 2003, the Henley Royal Regatta renamed the Women's Quadruple Sculls the "Princess Grace Challenge Cup." Prince Albert presented the prizes at the Regatta in 2004.

Following her mother's death, Caroline, Princess of Hanover assumed the presidency of The Princess Grace Foundation, and the organization continues Grace's aim of helping emerging theater, dance and film artists. An American branch of the non-profit organization is headquartered in New York. The Princess Grace Awards, a program of the Princess Grace Foundation-USA, has awarded more scholarships to more than 500 artists at more than 100 American institutions.

 The American Film Institute named Grace the 13th top female star of American cinema in June 1999.

Grace's colorful, glamorous life has been of interest to movie makers. In 1983, an American television film featuring Cheryl Ladd as Grace and Ian McShane as Prince Rainier debuted. In an article in the Feb. 21, 1983 edition of The New York Times, writer John J. O'Connor writes that the TV film has a "suffocating propriety that seeps through the project." He added that the film certainly will not offend anyone, but that it is likely not to interest anyone either.

A new major motion picture, *Grace of Monaco*, directed by Olivier Dahan and starring Nicole Kidman as Grace and Tim Roth as Rainier, is set for a May 2014 debut at the Cannes Film Festival.

The royal family of Monaco is reportedly upset about the movie, which Prince Albert told the *New York Post* "vilifies his father" as a "one-sided leader who is controlling over his wife." The *New York Post* report claims that producer Pierre-Ange Le Pogam denied the royal family a screening request by ignored the family's requests for changes to the script.

In January 2013, the Grimaldi family released a statement criticizing the movie and released a statement that said in part:

"The royal family wishes to stress that this film in no way constitutes a biopic. It recounts one rewritten and needlessly glamorized page in the history of Monaco and its family with both major historical inaccuracies and a series of purely fictional scenes."

Actress, princess, philanthropist, humanitarian, style icon, wife, mother, legend. Just what is the legacy of Grace Kelly? Why after all these years do we – both men and women, young and old alike – find her so fascinating? Her beauty? Certainly. The way she spoke and the effortless style and elegance she gave to whatever she was wearing? Absolutely.

Actor George Clooney, whose work has been compared with Grace's long-time friend and co-star Cary Grant, told People Magazine in 2013 that whenever he watches Grace emerge from the water in the film *To Catch a Thief*, he thinks she is the most beautiful woman he has ever seen.

But it is more than her beauty and elegance that intrigues us about Grace Kelly. Grace was someone who seemed to live her life on her own terms. She was able to get away from a dominating, sometimes unfeeling father and make her way as an individual in male-dominated world by playing by some of those same rules men lived by. Yet she did it in a way that showed warmth and openness. She was romantic and passionate, and she didn't always do what she was told.

Forever hounded by the press to comment on her reputation as being snobbish and cold, the people who knew Grace all seemed to find her to be the exact opposite. She was, after all, an actress, and the young star played her many parts well.

Perhaps her friend and costar Jimmy Stewart said it the best in the eulogy he gave at Grace's funeral:

"You know, I just love Grace Kelly. Not because she was a princess, not because she was an actress, not because she was my friend, but because she was just about the nicest lady I ever met. Grace brought into my life as she brought into yours, a soft, warm light every time I saw her, and every time I saw her was a holiday of its own. No question, I'll miss her, we'll all miss her, God bless you, Princess Grace.

Appendix: Grace's list of roles

Film

1956, High Society, Tracy Lord

1956, The Swan, Princess Alexandra

1955, To Catch a Thief, Frances Stevens

1954, Green Fire, Catherine Knowland

1954, The Country Girl, Georgie Elgin

1954 The Bridges at Toko-Ri, Nancy Brubaker

1954 Rear Window, Lisa Carol Fremont

1954 Dial M for Murder, Margot Mary Wendice

1953 Mogambo, Linda Nordley

1952 High Noon, Amy Fowler Kane

1951 Fourteen Hours, Louise Ann Fuller

Television

1948-1954 Kraft Theatre (TV Series)

　　The Thankful Heart (1954)

　　Boy of Mine (1953)

　　The Small House (1952)

　　The Cricket on the Hearth (1952)

　　Old Lady Robbins (1948)

　1950-1953 The Philco-Goodyear Television Playhouse (TV Series)

　　The Way of the Eagle (1953) ... Lucy Bakewell Audubon

　　Rich Boy (1952) Paula

　　The Sisters (1951)

　　Leaf out of a Book (1950)

　　Ann Rutledge (1950) Ann Rutledge

　　Bethel Merriday (1950) Bethel Merriday

1952-1953 Lux Video Theatre (TV Series)

　　The Betrayer (1953) Meg

　　A Message for Janice (1952) ... Janice

Life, Liberty and Orrin Dudley (1952) ... Beth

1950-1952 Studio One in Hollywood (TV Series)

The Kill (1952) Freda Clark

The Rockingham Tea Set (1950) Sara Mappin

1951-1952 Armstrong Circle Theatre (TV Series)

Recapture (1952)

City Editor (1952)

Brand from the Burning (1951)

Lover's Leap (1951)

1952 Goodyear Playhouse (TV Series)

Leaf Out of a Book (1952)

1952 Suspense (TV Series)

Fifty Beautiful Girls (1952)

1952 Robert Montgomery Presents (TV Series)

Candles for Theresa (1952) ... Therese

1950-1952 Lights Out (TV Series)

The Borgia Lamp (1952)

The Devil to Pay (1950)

1950-1952 Danger (TV Series)

Prelude to Death (1952)

The Sergeant and the Doll (1950)

1952 The Big Build Up (TV Movie)

Claire

1952 CBS Television Workshop (TV Series)

Don Quixote (1952) ... Dulcinea

1951 Nash Airflyte Theatre (TV Series)

A Kiss for Mr. Lincoln (1951) ... Mrs. Kennard

1951 The Prudential Family Playhouse (TV Series)

Berkeley Square (1951) ... Helen Pettigrew

1950 Somerset Maugham TV Theatre (TV Series)

Episode (1950)

1950 The Clock (TV Series)

Vengeance (1950)

1950 Big Town (TV Series)

The Pay-Off (1950)

1950 Actor's Studio (TV Series)

The Swan (1950) Princess Alexandra

The Token (1950)

The Apple Tree (1950)

1950 Believe It or Not (TV Series)

The Voice of Obsession (1950)

CPSIA information can be obtained at www.ICGtesting.com
Printed in the USA
LVOW01s1539260415

436154LV00028B/1562/P